Animal STORYBOOKS

Clown Fish Finds a Friend

Story by Rebecca Johnson
Photos by Steve Parish

GARETHSTEVENS
GS
PUBLISHING
A Member of the WRC Media Family of Companies

Please visit our web site at: www.garethstevens.com
For a free color catalog describing Gareth Stevens Publishing's list of high-quality books
and multimedia programs, call 1-800-542-2595 (USA) or 1-800-387-3178 (Canada).
Gareth Stevens Publishing's fax: (414) 332-3567.

Library of Congress Cataloging-in-Publication Data

Johnson, Rebecca, 1966–
    [Clever clownfish]
    Clown fish finds a friend / story by Rebecca Johnson; photos by Steve Parish. — North American ed.
        p. cm. — (Animal storybooks)
    Summary: A lonely clown fish leaves his anemone home and searches for a friend who looks just like himself.
    ISBN 0-8368-5969-3 (lib. bdg.)
    1. Anemonefishes—Juvenile fiction. [1. Anemonefishes—Fiction.] I. Parish, Steve, ill. II. Title.
PZ10.3.J683C1 2005
[E]—dc22
                                                  2005042629

First published as *Clever Clownfish* in 2003 by Steve Parish Publishing Pty Ltd, Australia.
Text copyright © 2003 by Rebecca Johnson. Photos copyright © 2003 by Steve Parish Publishing.
Series concept by Steve Parish Publishing.

This U.S. edition first published in 2006 by
Gareth Stevens Publishing
A Member of the WRC Media Family of Companies
330 West Olive Street, Suite 100
Milwaukee, Wisconsin 53212 USA

This edition copyright © 2006 by Gareth Stevens, Inc.

Gareth Stevens series editor: Dorothy L. Gibbs
Gareth Stevens cover and title page designs: Dave Kowalski

Printed in the United States of America

1 2 3 4 5 6 7 8 9 09 08 07 06 05

Little clown fish was feeling sad.
He was lonely.

It seemed that
the sea anemone
was his only friend.

The anemone's poisonous tentacles sting most fish, but the anemone liked clown fish and kept him safe.

There were other clown fish, of course.

Some were bright orange.

Some had blue stripes.

9

Some were black,
with little white tails.

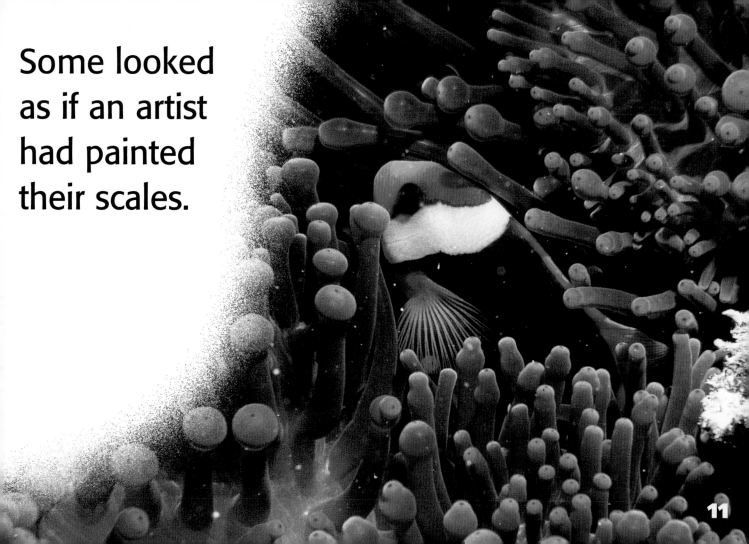

Some looked
as if an artist
had painted
their scales.

But clown fish wanted a friend just like himself. So, one day, he decided he would swim to the reef to find one.

At the reef, clown fish saw shiny, shimmering batfish,

14

a black-banded bannerfish
with a long white fin,

15

a yellow trumpetfish
with a very long nose,

and even some angelfish,
dancing among the coral.

He saw starfish so bright
they could light up the sky.

And some butterfly fish
went gliding by.

He saw cleaner fish
hard at work

helping other fish
show off their beauty.

But he did not see
any fish like himself.
Clown fish was starting
to think he might never
find a friend, when . . .

22

he saw a face, just like his, peeping shyly from inside an anemone. "Hello," said the other clown fish.

When little clown fish
swims, now, through the sea,
he swims with his friend
and their new family.